#HR
A SNARKY ADULT
COLORING BOOK
YOU CAN'T SPELL
Hero
WITHOUT HR

This Book Belongs To

______________________________

I'M IN
HR
I CAN'T FIX
CRAZY
BUT I CAN
DOCUMENT IT

DON'T
MAKE ME
Use My
HR
VOICE

I CAN WINE
ALL I WANT
I'M IN
HR

HUMAN
Resources
WE SOLVE
Problems
YOU DIDN'T KNOW
YOU HAD
IN WAYS YOU DON'T
UNDERSTAND

HR
NINJA

Keep
Calm
AND LET THE
HR MANAGER
Handle it

HR
CHAOS
COORDINATOR

YOU CAN'T SPELL
Hero
WITHOUT
HR

HR
POWERED BY
Coffee

THERE'S NO
Crying in
HR

What
HAPPENS IN
HUMAN RESOURCES
STAYS IN
Human
RESOURCES

HUMAN RESOURCES
THIS TIME IT'S PERSONNEL

I AM THE
Psychotic
HR PERSONNEL
EVERYONE WARNED
You About

World's
OKAYEST
HR
PERSONNEL

keep
CALM
and
CALL
HR

I'M HR
TO SAVE TIME LET'S
JUST ASSUME
THAT I'M NEVER WRONG

HR
MANAGER

GENUINE
&
TRUSTED
HR
PERSONNEL

i'm
REPORTING
this to
HR

Rule #1
THE HR MANAGER
IS ALWAYS RIGHT
Rule #2
IF THE HR MANAGER
IS WRONG REFER TO
Rule #1

PEOPLE IN
HR
ARE FABULOUS & MAGICAL
LIKE UNICORNS
ONLY
BETTER

Human
RESOURCES
BECAUSE FREAKING
MIRACLE WORKER
IS NOT AN OFFICIAL
JOB TITLE

SAFETY
First
DRINK WITH A
HUMAN RESOURCE
Specialist

I MAY NOT BE A
Superhero
BUT I'M A
Director
of
HUMAN
RESOURCE
SO CLOSE ENOUGH

Human
RESOURCES
Specialist

Made in the USA
Monee, IL
08 January 2021

56979536R00031